All You Need Is Less

Declutter Your Home Without Sacrificing Comfort And Coziness –

The Making of a Minimalist Life

Michelle Moore

michellembooks@gmail.com

Copyright © 2018 by Michelle Moore. All rights reserved.

No part of this publication may be reproduced, stored in a retrieval system, or transmitted in any form or by any means, electronic, mechanical, photocopying, recording, scanning or otherwise, except as permitted under Section 107 or 108 of the 1976 United States Copyright Act, without the prior written permission of the author.

Limit of Liability/ Disclaimer of Warranty: The author makes no representations or warranties with respect to the accuracy or completeness of the contents of this work and specifically disclaims all warranties, including without limitation warranties of fitness for a particular purpose. No warranty may be created or extended by sales or promotional materials. The advice and recipes contained herein may not be suitable for everyone. This work is sold with the understanding that the author is not engaged in rendering medical, legal or other professional advice or services. If professional assistance is required, the services of a competent professional person should be sought. The author shall not be liable for damages arising herefrom. The fact that an individual, organization of website is referred to in this work as a citation and/or potential source of further information does not mean that the author endorses the information the individual, organization to website may provide or recommendations they/it may make. Further, readers should be aware that Internet websites listed in this work might have changed or disappeared between when this work was written and when it is read.

For general information on the products and services or to obtain technical support, please contact the author.

Being a minimalist doesn't mean you have to throw out everything you love. Learn to apply minimalism to your life without sacrificing the coziness of your home.

Table Of Contents

Introduction 9
Chapter 1: Minimalism 17
Chapter 2: Comfy and Cozy 31
Chapter 3: Making Minimalism Cozy 43
Chapter 4: Swedish Death Cleaning 63
Chapter 5: How to Get Rid of Your Mess 75
Chapter 7: Organizing Tips 109
Chapter 8: Holiday Special 127
Final Thoughts 135
Other Books 139
Reference 141
Endnotes 145

Introduction

It was horrible.

What a start, right?

This is what crossed my mind too. I'd just arrived back at my New York apartment after almost six years of absence. Do you know that feeling when you return from somewhere, or you have your birthday and you arrive home and expect people to jump out from every part of the house, yelling "surprise" and jumping on you? There are balloons, trumpets, confetti...

Sure. What about spiders, dust, and a collapsed shelf? Ta-da! Welcome home, Mitch.

Let me wrap up the prelude to my life in a few sentences. I used to be the New York dream girl—fancy school, posh scholarship, strong-willed startup builder, wealthy parents (a mild, stay-at-home mom and a dad mean as a shark with a hangover, both in life and business. I always tried my best to impress him. I think I succeeded the most when I ran off chasing a web developer in Germany. I left everything behind in the name of eternal love, which ended much sooner than the relationship. Heartbroken—and totally broke—I ran away to backpack across the world, living as what some people today call a "digital nomad." I traveled from the deepest seas of Indonesia to the highest mountains of Peru. I ate scorpions in Cambodia and took selfies with a Parisian street dancer in front of the Eiffel tower.

Six years later, somewhat wiser, there I was on the porch of my messy little flat no one had used for a while. I hadn't rented it out, either, mostly because of the aforementioned clutter. Although I could have used the money, since at that time I was my family's disgraced only child.

I threw my backpack onto the floor since there was no free surface elsewhere. I went to turn the heating and electricity on, checked if my taps were still functional, and gratefully stated that at least I'd brought the trash out before "eloping." Now what?

Based on this brief introduction, you may think, "This woman is a total mess. Why should I even care about her book on... decluttering and living a cozy life? Really?"

You're right. I was a mess. I'd messed up everything humanly possible—my promising jobs, my degree at Columbia, my relationship with my family and friends, my relationships with men, and last but not least, my apartment.

But time passed and I grew. I'm actually very grateful for all the mistakes I've made in the past. Without them, I wouldn't be the person I am today. I would be much more ignorant to the world (even with a degree in my hand).

Do you feel like you've made lots of mistakes too? Who cares? Own them, deconstruct them, and build them back up as something educational, inspirational, and funny.

My big homecoming didn't happen last week, but two years ago. Since then, I've gotten a decent job, I'm on good terms again with my loved ones (although my father needed a little persuasion), and—most importantly, from this book's perspective—I have a home that is totally Pinterest-worthy. For those readers who are not familiar with Pinterest, let's just say it's the online version of *Elle Décor, Country Living, Architectural Digest,* and *Cosmopolitan.*

My napkin-flat looks spacious now. It is cozy and organized. I don't have many things left, but the things I have are meaningful or purposeful. I don't find any particular meaning in my frying pan, but it is quite handy when I want to make blueberry pancakes.

Now you know everything about me and my journey, so it's time to see what this book has in store for you.

What will you find here?

- First things first: I'll introduce you to the basics of minimalism. No nonsense—just minimalism.

- I'll take you through the significance of *hygge*, the Scandinavian method of being cozy, chilled, and happy.

- Then we'll discover the Swedish Death Cleaning Method—I promise the only corpses involved will be of old spiders you discard with your magazine collection from the 1980s.

- After the story time is over, it's time for hands-on work. I will tell you how I decluttered and downsized each living space—systematically and efficiently. I will guide you through each space in a flat—bedroom, closets, bathroom, kitchen, living room, and garage. There will be no survivors.

- Once the house is nice and airy, it's time to find a better place for everything that remains. I will help you to create the home you wish to have with simple organizing tips and folding methods.

- Magic time. When the clutter is removed and the rest is organized, it is time to add some magic to make your house a home. I will give you some de facto decoration tips, but also some advice that goes beyond pure material goods, like how to breathe life into your living space— figuratively and literally. Sounds uncommonly spiritual from everything you may already think about me. No worries. My tips are not crazy spiritual, just mildly spiritual. Tips spiritual and non-spiritual people can both enjoy.

Without further ado, please enjoy my book made to help you live simply and cozily.

Chapter 1: Minimalism

Minimalism is currently very trendy, and for good reason. Getting rid of items in your household that may no longer have meaning or purpose helps you to reduce that choking feeling of dealing with too much physically and mentally. Studies have shown that when people err on the side of minimalism, something amazing happens—they suddenly invite better enrichment into their lives.

Thankfully, you don't have to set up a huge garage sale and sell everything you own to be considered a minimalist. Clearing out some of your physical items is surely helpful, but it doesn't mean you have to live out in the woods with non-perishable food and a tent. Adopting minimalism can be fun, leaving your place completely cozy, if it is done well.

What is minimalism? This is the question many people ask. Some people think minimalism is some fad, a new trend that will slowly go away—something pop stars like Madonna started that slowly spilled over into the houses of the common populace. Unfortunately, minimalism has some negative connotations attached to it too. Some think it is a scam. People say it is completely unnecessary for common people, or that it's just a hobby for rich hipsters. Others criticize minimalism as being hidden consumerism—you throw away your old things just to buy fewer, but more expensive stuff, like red wood cup-holders covered with organic polish, or some similar crap.

Clearly, if minimalism was any or every of the options listed above, I wouldn't write a book on it to try to convince you to adopt it. Minimalism, if used advantageously, isn't a fad. It's rather a lifestyle, a state of mind, a chill way of approaching life, a healthy relationship with objects, and an even healthier with people. If you think of minimalism as being restrictive or prohibitive, you're not approaching it in a constructive way. Minimalism can and should help you find freedom in your life.

Joshua Fields Millburn and Ryan Nicodemus, the authors and owners of the website *The Minimalists*, have helped millions of people over the years to better their lives and find freedom through living a minimalist lifestyle. These two minimalists look at the minimalist lifestyle as a method of achieving freedom. Choosing to be a minimalist can help you to find freedom from our haughty culture and rise above your own negative feelings.[i]

Having a ton of stuff can cause guilt, fear, worry, and anxiety. Having some material possessions isn't a bad thing, but giving too much of your emotions and attention to the material can lead you to a life of discontent, and ultimately emptiness. If all your thoughts and goals revolve around getting a new car, phone, or dress, you'll never experience deep satisfaction. I don't know if you've noticed it, but buying things doesn't provide even a fraction of the satisfaction you think it will.

Not to mention that the more stuff you have, the more you have to clean, take care of, and invest more time in. Adopting a minimalist approach in your life can help you get more time, discover and invest more in your passions, find what your mission in life is, experience freedom, create more, focus on more important things, and grow.

In my understanding, minimalism is the mindset that helps you realize what has value in your life now and possibly in the future. It helps you let go of things that are not serving you, not helping you in any way, and it doesn't only apply to physical items. Minimalism can apply to all areas of your life like your beliefs and relationships. You cannot strip down your life with a line of where minimalism can and can not pervade. Moreover, one can call herself a minimalist by heart if she adopts the philosophy in her external and internal world simultaneously.

There is no standard amount of belongings that will suddenly make you a minimalist. For example, just because someone owns only 100 items, it doesn't mean that he is a minimalist. He can be an extremist, or he can be very poor and owning only 100 things is not a choice, but rather a condition. But if someone has 100 things for the purpose of finding inner peace and living simply, he can be considered a minimalist.

There is no one-size-fits-all set of characteristics for minimalism. It is more about finding out what works for you. Think of this philosophy as the mental crutch that helps you determine what does and what doesn't have value in your life. You can learn to better appreciate the things that you have, which helps you to become more grateful, with your expectations in check.

The Origins of Minimalism

Minimalism started off in post-World War II Western art. More commonly, it used to describe art that became popular in the 1960s and 1970s in America. It was the modern art movement that stripped away the traditional business of art and left things simple and clean looking. Often minimalism is considered to be opposed to abstract expressionism, another art movement born in the aftermath of World War II. In contrast to minimalism, abstract expressionism aimed to describe the horrors of war in an intense, often surreal, colorful, subconscious-driven way. In other words, it was the complete opposite of minimalism. Minimalism spilled over to influence music, visual arts, modern design, and architecture over the decades.

Today, in its basic form, minimalism means reducing things to be simpler. This can take on a whole multitude of ideas when applied to your life. Some people want the minimalist designs which are found in housing décor with strong angles and easy to follow patterns. Others want to declutter everything they own and get rid of a majority of their belongings. And others, well, they want to apply minimalism to their emotional life, simplifying the way they live.

There isn't a right or wrong way to do minimalism. Minimalism is about the personal journey. Whatever feels necessary to you is the reason you should be adopting this philosophy. You might be reading this book and thinking about all the possessions in your bedroom. Maybe you have clothes and shoes strewn across the closet that you are hoping to get rid of, maybe your car looks more like a second home than a vehicle that takes you to work, or maybe you feel that you have too many people in your life and you don't get the chance to be with yourself.

Maybe you are already a minimalist at heart. Maybe you are thinking about everything you own and don't think there's much to get rid of. The question is, how do you feel? Are you overwhelmed with what's going on in your life, whether it is too many clothes, too many work commitments, or too many surface friends? Do you feel a sense of calm and peace, or do you feel distressed and consumed by chaos on a day-to-day basis?

Before you get started purging through your life, there are some concerns people bring up with minimalism. In fact, these concerns may be echoing in your mind right now. Don't worry, it is natural to have them. They have been present since the dawn of minimalism.

For one, many people think minimalism is something only wealthy people do. Only they can afford to get rid of their things because if they need to, they can simply go out and buy them again. The pre-modern minimalists of the past have usually been wealthy bachelors.

As I mentioned before, the poorest individuals are hardly the true minimalists. They own very little mostly because they can't afford more, and they cherish what they have by caring for it to the best of their ability.

If getting rid of something in your life causes you stress, you have to ask yourself, why? Most likely, the reason is one of the following: We are so focused on having a certain amount of items in our lives that getting rid of them feels like getting rid of something of ourselves, or we feel bad about getting rid of stuff because we think that more stuff give more security. Another reason that makes a knot in your stomach when you think about discarding can be emotional attachment, or the sense of obligation to keep something. Think about that old decoration your great aunt gave you. Sure, it's ugly as sin, but you have to keep it in case she ever asks about it, right?

Not exactly, but that brings us to the second problem with minimalism. Even if you are purging stuff throughout your house, you are still thinking about the stuff. You could be stuffing yourself at a buffet, or you could be starving on a diet, but either way, you're going to be thinking about food.

When we decide to clean out our lives, we often refill those holes with other things. The shelves we empty may just serve for holding future clutter if we get stuck focusing only on the objects. The key to minimalism is not letting material things take up your thoughts and time. You may get a thrill from cleaning out your closet, but if you clean it out just to jam other, newer clothes in, it was a wasted effort. How can you avoid falling back to your pre-decluttering state? I will talk about it later in the book.

Minimalism can be a great lifestyle, but when it is taken to the extreme, it can haunt you more so than living normally. The key to a stress-free minimalist life is dedicating time to cleansing your personal belongings and everything else in your life, and then don't think too much about it. Don't stress over the tiniest details, and don't fall prey to perfectionism.

The focus of this book is to help you redesign your lifestyle in a minimalist way. I want to help you to create a cozy and simple life, one you can go home to without stress and clutter, but still have it feel like a home. You want to be surrounded by people and things that matter to you, that are important, and that will last you a long time.

Minimalism helps you balance the curse of diminishing returns

Let minimalism extend to other parts of your life; if you have a few great friends who care about you and listen to you, you won't need the 50 other friends who you call only once a year and send a Christmas card to. Those types of friends waste precious time that you could be using for the people who really care about you. After all, the things that matter most in life have diminishing returns the more of them you have.

Think about it. Having one true friend is truly special. Having two is even better. But when you have 20 pals, getting the 21st won't make a cathartic difference in your life. Hearing "I love you" from your significant other once a month can mean a lot. Hearing it twice feels lovely as well. But hearing it twice a day will force the confession to sink to the level of "good morning" and "what will we have for lunch?" There are diminishing returns in everything—the 10th dress, the 50th shoe, the third hamburger, traveling, reading books on a topic, etc.

Let's take this journey together. Let me help you become a minimalist while still keeping your home comfy and cozy.

Chapter 2: Comfy and Cozy

Let me paint you a picture: You walk up to a home that is as tall as a small skyscraper, lined with reflective glass. The grass outside is nonexistent; instead, it has been replaced with a concrete-colored gravel that accompanies the metal stair railing. When you walk into the house, the smell is clean and dust-free. The floors are concrete, the staircase is straight and glass, and the view from the window is a mile long. One piece of artwork hangs on the wall. It is a modern piece with sharp angles and no color. In fact, the whole house is decorated in varying shades of black, white, and gray. You marvel at how beautiful and clean the home is.

What I just described is the epitome of a minimalist's home. When people think of minimalist designs, they rarely think to associate it with coziness. Instead they assume the minimalist lifestyle is reflected in fancy modern houses that have no color in them at all. Everything is sterile, and it resembles a hospital room rather than a home that is loved and lived in.

Let's be honest, we tend to associate minimalism with ultra-modernism. Living minimally is a very modern way of life, after all. But it doesn't have to mean you live in a fancier version of a hospital or office building. There's no reason that minimalism has to mean cold and distant.

If you decide to keep only a few things, it doesn't mean they all have to be purchased at some fancy department store. Your sole blanket could be one that was knit by your grandmother, your artwork on the walls could be photos of your family, or you could have candles that line your home with your favorite scent. All of these things can still be part of a minimalist lifestyle.

Remember when as a child you begged for a toy and you got it? I remember that I really wanted this Barbie playhouse. I was probably only seven or eight, but the thought of having this Barbie house made me so excited. I was so pumped up when my birthday came.

The morning of my birthday, I received the Barbie playhouse and couldn't wait to use it! However, I quickly forgot about it when my mom brought out her famous chocolate cake. I was dressed in fleece, watching the snowflakes fall to the ground outside, surrounded by the lights of the candles on the cake. My mother continued making breakfast, which turned out to be pancakes, thick slices of ham, and roasted potatoes.

After eating breakfast, we stayed in our pajamas all day and watched Disney movies. I got the toy I wanted, but the whole experience of my birthday that year was special to me. Whether it's a cozy winter day where you cuddled in a blanket with a loved one, or a summer day where you played on the beach with your family, we can all think of a time that we felt warm, secure, and safe.

In Scandinavia, one of the coldest places in the world, people have a cultural practice called *hygge*. *Hygge* means "wellbeing," but many Scandinavians use it to describe an almost meditative state that they immerse themselves in. For them, there's nothing better than a steaming cup of hot cocoa, apple cider, or a mug of coffee. Can you feel it? The warm steam tendrils flitting around our faces provide us with the utmost comfort. It is something we all dream about when winter comes around. Hygge is a little like that.[ii]

You want to create a warm physiological response, which is what hygge promotes. It is a sense of contentment and put-togetherness. When you thought of a family dinner with your parents and grandparents, or about the lazy afternoon sun at the beach, how did you feel? While it isn't nearly as good as actually experiencing one of those activities, thinking about something cozy can promote a good feeling similar to the action itself. You might relax more, smile more, and enjoy the everyday things in your life. This feeling is hygge.

Hygge can fit into a minimalist lifestyle because it focuses on keeping things cozy while keeping them simple. When you want to promote more hygge in your life, surround yourself with things that make you feel good and cozy. Remember the curse of diminishing returns. Having one cozy mug is special; having 12 is not.

The great thing about hygge is it can be used mentally and physically. Thinking about cozy times can help you feel better, and it can also trigger your brain to release oxytocin. Once these feel-good chemicals are released, your brain's frontal lobe is engaged and you feel ready to take on the day. You are more focused and empowered.

Hygge can also be used as a bit of an indulgence. Eat that slice of cake, treat yourself to something you really want, but always remember to keep moderation. Chill out, relax, and surround yourself with things that make you feel good.

This is completely different than the average American lifestyle. We are always on the go. We care so much about achievement and the next big thing that we often forget to stop and enjoy the things we work so hard for.

The countries that practice hygge are often known to have some of the happiest people in the world. Is this because of the practice? Maybe, maybe not. However, their laidback personalities are clearly helping them to be happy. The trick has to be that rather than focusing on perfection, they immerse themselves in experiences and allow themselves to make mistakes.

If you identify yourself as someone who doesn't get that warm and fuzzy feeling on the inside often, it is time to give hygge a try. Caution: If you are hiding from your problems by trying to practice hygge, you're doing it wrong.

In actuality, the super laidback and the overachievers are at opposite ends of the spectrum. You want to focus on being somewhere in the middle. Incorporating hygge into your life can help you feel good and fulfilled without having to buy a bunch of things, can help simplify your life, and can help you see what you really care about. If anything, hygge should show you that nothing that truly matters in life is actually perfect.

Imagine hygge as a warm and comforting hug. But when you hug someone, you aren't getting just the physical touch from it. You are going to benefit from warm and fuzzy feelings, comfort, caring, safety, and a sense of belonging. Hygge can be a scarf knit by your late grandmother—it may have some holes and discoloration on it, but made with so much affection. Hygge is whatever feeling that scarf triggers in you—deep love, selfless caring, unconditional acceptance, tireless attention. This is what thinking of my grandmother would make me feel. It feels warm. I feel happy.

The feeling of hygge can be created by a minimalistic lifestyle. You can start by creating a cozy atmosphere around you. Choose things that have meaning for you and discard the meaningless. For example, keep the nice kitty cup you got from your mom instead of the random monochromatic IKEA coffee mugs strewn across your kitchen. Decorate your home with candles and family photos instead of knickknacks. Create a place where you can feel at home.

To me, this meant recreating my grandparents' home—with much less clutter, of course. For dishes, I kept some of my late grandmothers' personal items. They don't look as nice as the latest kitchen décor from Walmart, but they make me happy. I love using the same tools my granny did. Are they perfect? No, not by far. But they still make me happier than any silver spoon. I'm so grateful that I could also have my late grandparents' coffee table. I chose furniture for my living room that's similar in color to what they had, and I made sure to hang a few handmade bird figures around, just like my granny did. This is hygge for me. What is it for you?

Perhaps the biggest part about hygge that goes hand in hand with minimalism is being grateful for what you have. Hygge is all about appreciating the small things life has to offer. The simple pleasures in life are more than enough to put you into the happy-cozy zone if you receive them with gratitude. Immerse yourself in these experiences. Put down the TV remote and cell phone and focus on what is in front of you. Enjoy the blanket your mom knit you and relish in the scent of your favorite pine-scented candle. Draw yourself a bath or snuggle in your bed. You don't need a ton of things to make your home cozy.

Finding pleasure in the things you have not only keeps your life clutter-free, it also helps you feel comfortable in your home.

Chapter 3: Making Minimalism Cozy

You've read about hygge and you want that feeling in your life, but you don't know exactly how to mix it with a minimalist routine. Coziness sounds great, but maybe you look around your house and think, "Oh, no, there's nothing cozy around here. I need to go shopping." Or you think that cozy must mean cluttered—maybe because the places where you felt cozy as a child were cluttered. Let me tell you this—it was not the place, it were the people who made you feel cozy. My grandparents' home was very cluttered, but it also felt very cozy. When they passed away and I returned to their home, nothing about it felt cozy anymore. It seemed like a bitterly empty space. Nothing changed in the house itself; the only difference was that my loved ones were not there anymore.

Isn't it true that a hug from someone you love is so much better than a blanket wrapped around you? It seems like a nice down comforter would feel so much warmer, but it doesn't. There's nothing better than a hug from a grandparent, the first kiss from your child, or holding hands with your partner. The reasons behind this are quite simple: Coziness seems to come from our environment, but it really comes from within us. We create our coziness. Therefore, I'm going to challenge you right now with a cozy project of the year.

Each month, pledge to do something cozy to bring yourself that good feeling. Your wellbeing comes from within, and it can happen by growing that warmth and coziness within your heart. If you don't have ideas of your own, don't worry. For each month, I have a guideline you can follow that will help increase that hygge feeling within you.

January: Who here hates January? I don't like this month, I will be honest with you. All my winter depression happens in January. Sure, the New Year is a fun celebration, but after that, real life comes back. There isn't an endless slew of holidays to look forward to, and the magic of Christmas seems like it's gone forever. January feels like when your favorite series is over: "My life has no purpose now." You might be trudging back to work, starting exams at university, trying to lose all the holiday weight you put on, and on top of it all, you're probably broke from all the spending you did at Christmas. If you live on the Northern Hemisphere, it is also cold outside. It's not a heartwarming month.

Here's the challenge for this month: Let's try to extend that Christmas magic just a little bit longer. Keep your Christmas lights up. Whether you have them on your house or they are decorating the inside of your home, turn them on at night and cuddle up to the extended magic of Christmas.

You don't need to be Christian or religious at all to celebrate Christmas. Because of Western influence, the Japanese have started to celebrate Christmas, but of course, they don't celebrate the birth of Jesus. For them, Christmas is a mish-mash of Valentine's Day and Thanksgiving. They give presents to their significant others and come together for a family dinner.

If you don't celebrate Christmas in any form, your challenge is to get a few candles and light them every evening. Be careful not to leave your candles unattended, but let your soul to be warmed by the gentle dance of the flames.

February: Whether you are watching snowflakes fall or running your fingers through the sand, February is a time for some warm drinks. It's the shortest month of the year, so let's get a little bit indulgent. We are going to do a cocoa challenge. Have a mug of hot chocolate every day. But hey, if cocoa isn't your thing, you can also do herbal tea. If you are lucky enough to have warm weather in February, drink iced cocoa or tea

The trick to this month is not feeling guilty about your cocoa intake. If you want to keep your health up, there's a great way to still have your cocoa without feeling bad about it. The hot cocoa in the store is filled with a bunch of unhealthy ingredients, and it doesn't even taste great! Instead, make my grandmother's recipe. It is delicious, healthy-ish, and the raw cocoa is full of antioxidants!

> 1 cup milk, divided
> 1 Tbs. raw cocoa powder
> Sweetener to taste

- In a medium saucepan, bring ¾ cup milk to a boil. In your mug, mix together the cocoa powder and remaining milk until no lumps remain. Once the milk has reached a boil, stir in the cocoa powder and milk mixture. You can add a bit of honey, stevia, or vanilla and sugar, if you desire. Take it off the heat, pour into your mug, and enjoy! (You can use more cocoa powder if you'd like to make your drink more chocolatey.)

March: The winter is slowly melting away, and soon spring is going to be right before our eyes! The challenge this month is to get in touch with nature and wake her up. It's time to make your environment a little brighter by planting some flowers. Flowers can be planted inside or outside.

If you want a one-time investment, buy some tulips. Not only are they fairly cheap at farmers markets, but they keep growing every year around spring. Once the flower has wilted, keep the root and watch it bloom again next year! It is an easy way to make things a bit brighter.

April: Hopefully it is warming up where you live, because it is time to appreciate some nature. Having nature in your home by planting some flowers is not enough. Welcome to your nature challenge month.

This month, do something outside every single day. You can go for a hike, a walk, or just sit outside and enjoy the weather for a few minutes. Meditating in the warmth of the sun is a great way to show your appreciation of nature.

May: Summer is just around the corner. It might already be warm where you live, or the last bit of coolness might be blowing through before it turns into a warm breeze. Because the warmest part of the year is near, it is time to treat yourself.

Don't go crazy, it isn't time to bring a bunch of stuff into your home or empty your savings account. This month, choose one thing that enhances your self-care. Been avoiding the dentist? Go for that Hollywood smile. Desperately need a new hairdo? Go to the salon. Buy yourself a face mask or grab a massage. There's no need to go crazy, but do at least one of these things for yourself.

June: The challenge for this month is easy and fun. The weather is warm, and it is time to plan a get-together. One rule, though: no technology allowed. Invite over your closest friends and family. You can do something simple like a barbecue, a pool party, or you could do a fun board game night!

July: Can you believe that the year is already halfway through? Time flies! July is all about introspection. Think about everything that has happened in the past six months and find something you are grateful for. Actually, find three things you are grateful for. Pull out a slip of paper and write three separate people a little note expressing your gratitude for what they have done for you. Alternatively, you could bake them a treat or muffin along with the card to show them how much you care.

August: The summer is almost over, so this month's challenge is to dedicate some of your time to your community. Volunteer for a day at the soup kitchen, feed the homeless, or spend a day picking up trash. Or you can help a neighbor with something or adopt a pet, if you want one. This is the best time to get the older pets who are left behind after the spring's breeding season.

September: It's fall! This is the month all pumpkin spice-flavored things arrive in stores. Cozy items surround you every single day this month, so it is time to enjoy something that is already provided for you.

Go out with some friends and enjoy some fall-related activities! You can pick up fall leaves together and make some decorations for your home. These nature-themed decorations won't last forever, so they will not clutter your home, but they sure are fun to create and are nice while they last!

October: It's the month of Halloween! Arguably the start of the holiday season, October is a great time to host a Halloween party with some of your friends and family. Get together to carve pumpkins, play board games, make your costumes, and have a pumpkin pie contest.

November: With Thanksgiving approaching, it is time to learn some new recipes. Bake a new batch of muffins and fill your body with all of those delicious carbs! It is time to indulge and treat yourself to the holiday season. The challenge is to try a recipe you have never tried before.

December: Do you even need a reason to get cozy this month? Your challenge now is to spread your own warmth around. Be kind to strangers every day and make it a goal to declutter your home. Get rid of the things that no longer serve a purpose and donate them to a charity. Your gently used items could be the holiday difference to someone else, and it feels great to know your old things are going where they will be loved.

These little monthly tasks can increase your own warm and fuzzy feelings within your soul! You'll feel truly blessed and happy whenever you do these activities. I'm sure you've already done most of them at some point in your life. They were cool, weren't they? Don't let these precious opportunities slip by. Take action and embrace them. Create the world you'd love to live in.

Beyond these monthly challenges, there are things you can do daily to increase your general wellbeing.

If you live in a colder climate, coziness comes quite easy. When you search "cozy" on the internet, you are bombarded with photos of people wrapped up in warm blankets in front of the fire as the delicate snowflakes brush the windows outside. You probably fill your days with thick blankets and warm socks, homemade coffee mugs, candlelight, and cookies baked fresh in the oven. You can also dim your lights. Light some candles throughout your home (but make sure to keep them in holders so nothing burns), or adjust your own lighting.

If you live where it stays pretty mild or warm, don't be discouraged. There are still a lot of ways you can increase the coziness of your home. You can also dim your lights, listen to audiobooks, or put on some soft music. Or you can take advantage of what most people in cold climates don't have access to—the outdoors! Engaging in nature activities is a great way to increase the coziness of your life. For example, you could have a picnic with your family. Make a sweet picnic blanket from old shirts or kitchen cloths, use your mason jars to hold sauces, and pack it all in your picnic basket. Not only can this increase the time you spend with your family, but it somehow could be just what you needed to do. You end up leaving the picnic feeling whole and complete.

I have traveled throughout the tropics, and homes there felt very cozy. Coziness gets a different definition, of course, but you definitely feel it. The large windows, big balconies, and the open air is all part of being comfy. You can also add one or two vintage pillows, a nice painting for decoration, and some beautiful candlelight.

If you are struggling with how to increase your coziness, I've put together a list of 10 quick things you can do to ensure you live a minimalist life that is comfortable and cozy. Follow these steps below.

1. Have a no-screen night each week or each month, depending on what you can handle. Replace the screen with a paperback book, soft music, cooking a new recipe, or time with friends.
2. Feeling blue? Buy a new candle! It is an inexpensive way to satisfy your shopping urge, and it will make you happy when you smell your favorite scent wafting through the house.

3. Have a movie night with family and friends. Ask each person to write the title of a movie they'd like to watch on a piece of paper. Throw them all in a basket. Have a rock-paper-scissors competition and the winner picks a movie from the basket. Watch the movie with some ginger tea or hot cocoa.
4. Sunday? Make it a pajama day. One Sunday each month, pledge to wear your pajamas all day long. Do stuff at home, relax, and enjoy the cozy environment you've created for yourself.
5. Cold outside? Go out! Just don't forget your fluffy scarf and hooded coat. Oh, and don't forget those possum-merino gloves the aggressive New Zealand merchants sold you, you gullible

tourist. Go out. Enjoy the warmth. That's why you keep that gigantic scarf in your closet, after all.

6. Doodle. When you have an hour of free time, do some doodling. If you have inspiration, even better. If you don't, just use the bored kid technique—pull the pen up and down, left and right. Now look at it. Try to guess what the heck it is and fill in the missing parts. Once, I created a cow with cockroach legs and a Persian cat tail. What was it called in the Greek mythology again? Cowroachusa?

7. Do a no-complaint day. If you are a notorious whiner, it will be difficult, but try. Each time you complain, do 10 jumping jacks. Yes, even in the middle of the metro station. Don't worry,

some of the other people are much crazier than you.

8. Do a complaint day. Oh, yeah. Just let it out. Complain for a day. Complain so much that you start considering it funny. Complain about the good stuff too. Make up dialogues in your head about how you complain about a perfectly manufactured cappuccino. It's the tip of the heart illustration on the foam. It's curved slightly left—which has to mean bad luck. Complaining a lot opens your eyes to how ridiculous it is to complain about other mundane things. Try to keep it in mind the next time your complaints are fueled by your own entitlement.

9. Say no to something. No comment needed.

10. Do one of the following activities: ice skate, go to a sauna, go on a hike, or go to a café with a fireplace (or have a coffee in front of yours) with some friends.

Chapter 4: Swedish Death Cleaning

My grandparents were anything but minimalists. Coming from the age of the Great Depression, they felt like they had to hold onto *everything*. No, literally, I mean everything. When they passed away, I was heartbroken. When the family was read the will, my grandma had arranged for a cleaning company to come to the house and clean it all. My whole family was appalled. We were not going to let some random cleaning company get rid of all the precious family heirlooms in their home!

However, when we all came to the house to clean, we quickly called that cleaning company back. Eight cat statues later, I knew my grandma was being smart when she arranged for that cleaning company. My grandma, being the saint that she was, had boxed up things she thought we would want. Why she didn't get rid of all the other stuff in the house is beyond me! I was just grateful I didn't have to go through it. I was left with some beautiful family heirlooms in the box labeled with my name, and the cousin that was always troublesome was left with my grandma's favorite cat. I kept some furniture and appliances—most of them are in my home now. Considering that cat was about as old as grandma, I made out pretty well.

Here's the thing—my grandma was a total hoarder. Loved her to pieces, but her arrangement for the cleaning company in her will just goes to show she was aware of her problem. It made me think of why we all hold onto so much stuff. I mean, we are all going to die at some point, and someone else is going to have to clean up after us. There are families everywhere that are stuck for days, weeks, or months, trying to go through their loved ones' belongings and trying to find the one item they would want to keep in remembrance of those who passed. Of course this process involves a lot of suffering, guilt, and sorrow. I mean, when a loved one dies, how could you throw out even the smallest, most insignificant item she ever owned? Those things are all that you have left of her. Chances are that by heart, you'd rather keep everything.

Margareta Magnusson has an idea that could just help all of us in this cleaning process that happens when our loved ones pass. She talks about a Swedish practice called "Döstädning," or death-cleaning. The word sounds morbid, sure, but it actually makes a lot of sense. Magnusson said that she's been cleaning her house routinely for the past 40 years as if she were preparing for her death. She quite enjoys the practice, and she suggests that everyone should do it.[iii]

Her motto is that if you do not love it, you lose it. Keeping hold of things that don't bring you any joy is making your house cluttered. While you may not mind the clutter, someone else who has to clean up after your death sure will. Death-cleaning is different than the act of cleaning up after a person who has died. When you are death-cleaning your own things, it can bring a lot of joy and happiness. You get to go through old memories and throw out things that don't mean anything to you. Not only does it save your relatives time after you pass away, but it reminds you what you have and what you do not need.[iv]

If we could all think like Margareta Magnusson, we might not have so much stuff. Death is a natural thing, but many of us feel awkward talking or thinking about it. While it may not be your dinner conversation of choice, having a death-cleaning talk in your family can be really beneficial. My grandma was a complete hoarder. She loved keeping vintage items, and she regularly went online to purchase knickknacks she thought were cool.

Your death-cleaning talk doesn't have to be morbid—it can be light and fun! You should talk to your loved ones about cleaning up after yourself. Talk about the importance of decluttering so that what's left are important and meaningful objects.

If you are reading this and think that death-cleaning sounds like a great idea, you might want to slow down. And if you are afraid of death-cleaning, you don't need to be. For one, death-cleaning isn't some all-day purging event. It's not working you dead by cleaning your whole house. The Swedish death-cleaning's aim is to slowly, but steadily, clean your house as the years go by. You can start this whenever you want, but ideally, it should have been started by the time you are in your 40s. Not that you should expect your death in the next half century, but you will naturally better if you keep your surroundings easily cleanable and neat.

The first step to death-cleaning is to talk to others about it. You are going to need someone to hold you accountable, and just saying it out loud helps you to follow through with it.

The second step is to not be afraid of death-cleaning. Just because you practice death-cleaning does not mean you are tempting fate for an early death. It's actually a very enjoyable and fun experience. You get to go through all of your old memories. Things that mean something to you, like old photographs, are so fun to look at, and it actually enhances the whole process. There aren't too many people who get to go through their sentimental items and pick out the most important things.

If you're struggling with the items in your house, there are some important and easy questions to ask yourself. First of all, consider how others feel about your things. Ask yourself: Am I going to use this item ever again (or how often will I use them)? If you are holding onto your cheerleader pom-poms, well, they'll hardly be of any use to anyone. Will my belongings make my loved ones happy after I am gone? Or will these belongings place a burden on them? No one wants to burden their loved ones after they go to the Happy Hunting Grounds.

Death-cleaning can take up a good chunk of your time, and going through sentimental items is going to take you on a trip down Memory Lane. You could spend days or weeks yourself just going through sentimental items! Because of this, it's best to leave your sentimental items for last.

When you start death-cleaning, start with your wardrobe. For some reason, we just aren't as attached to our clothes as other items in our house. Don't feel guilty getting rid of your clothes. If you haven't worn it in a year, it is time to get rid of it. And if you've only worn the item once or twice in a year, it is best to get rid of it in that case too. Stick to the pieces in your wardrobe that you wear over and over again. There is no reason to hold onto clothes that no longer fit, are out of style, or just don't get used very often. These items are taking up space in your closet, your mind, and your life. Your wardrobe purge can be done much faster than your sentimental purge. Once your wardrobe is done, appreciate the items left over and *do not* go shopping!

Another tip for death-cleaning is to not display items that you do not like around your house. If your sibling gave you a sculpture that you absolutely hate, don't display it. If you proudly put it up in your house, that gives others ideas for what they should buy you. Believe me, I know this one from experience. One day you are cringing when you open that box with the chicken statue in it, and the next year you are plastering a fake smile on your face when you open three more chicken statues. If I hadn't displayed that horrible chicken statue in the first place, I wouldn't have gotten three more the next year! And then I feel horrible throwing them away, so I am left with chicken statue after chicken statue. I create and decorate with handmade little birds, not chickens.

I don't know why you people assume I like them. I honestly don't know where do you even find them, but please, stop gifting them to me! Low point, sorry.

Learn from my mistake and don't display items you don't like. This will help prevent you from getting random knickknacks that you just have to throw away later.

Last, but certainly not least, Magnusson says that death-cleaning should be rewarded. Purging a bunch of your stuff isn't always the most fun idea for a Friday night. Because of this, you should reward yourself for the efforts. Go grab a bite to eat with your friend at the new restaurant down the road, go see a movie, or do something you love. The key here is absolutely *no* shopping. You don't want to accumulate more stuff and have to start your death-cleaning all over again.

Swedish death-cleaning is similar, but different from Marie Kondo's view on minimalism. Neither of them are wrong, but using both methods could help you pare down what you have lying around the house. When Marie Kondo wrote *The Life-Changing Magic of Tidying,* she never could have guessed she would be world-famous. The book focused on only keeping items that bring you joy. If the item didn't bring you joy, you should get rid of it. This is a great way to start your minimalism journey, but death-cleaning makes you think beyond yourself. You need to ask, "Will anyone be better off if I save this?"

In *The Gentle Art of Swedish Death Cleaning*[v], Margareta Magnusson asks readers to consider the burden they put on others. We might say that our crossword puzzles bring us joy, but your loved ones aren't going to be any better off by you leaving your crossword puzzles lying around. It is best to think of both yourself and others when death-cleaning. This is the perfect start to thinking about minimalism in your life, but you still keep things cozy by keeping what is most important to you. Not only will you feel better about decluttering your house, but your loved ones will thank you as well.

Chapter 5: How to Get Rid of Your Mess

We all have some clutter lying around the house; that's normal. However, there can come a moment in life when you feel that you've had enough, you are choking on it, and you wish to get rid of it. I hope this moment just arrived for you. Ready to roll your sleeves up and do some actual work? Let's begin!

What is clutter? In its simplest terms, it is whatever you're keeping that isn't useful, purposeful, or emotionally valuable for you. Clutter isn't essential, and it isn't adding any value to your life. Little knickknacks, old gifts, books you'll never read, expired foods, old files, outgrown clothes—the list goes on and on.

Decluttering can save you from living a stressful life. Clutter causes a lot of stress. It is just demoralizing to step into a house that's as crowded as a swimming pool in China during summer. Not to mention the effort cleaning all the useless things requires—dusting, organizing, moving them around. When you get rid of things that no longer serve a purpose, your life opens up. A big amount of stress and obligations fall off your shoulders. You are making space in your life for the important things that add joy and value. If you're still skeptical about how decluttering can help you out, it's time to see it from science's side.

A research study conducted at UCLA at the Center on Everyday Lives and Family found that clutter can directly affect your mental health. Your self-esteem and mood can be dependent on the clutter in your home. When a person has more household objects, their levels of stress are higher. Household objects and stress hormones seem to be correlated.[vi]

When you reduce the amount of items in your house, you get better control over your life. Who wouldn't want more control in their lives? Human beings, by nature, love control. Whether you consider yourself a control freak or not, deep down, we all love to be a bit controlling at times. So no matter which way you look at it, decluttering now and then is going to make your life more balanced.

It's time to buckle down and get rid of your clutter. While you could do an all-out purge of your household items, it is best to start with a few basic steps to ensure your cleaning process is efficient.

First of all, before you start going through your household items faster than a thief in a store, you should create very specific goals about how much and what exactly you wish to downsize. Have a plan and a final vision in your mind on how you wish your house to look. A clear vision lessens the chance of frustration, procrastination, and stress during the process. We like to know what to expect in life, and throwing yourself into a room without a plan is akin to jumping into a tank with hungry sharks.

Draw a picture of the rooms in your house and try to guess how much clutter you have in each. You don't have to stress about the picture you draw; it can literally look like a bunch of circles with the name of each room in the middle of the circle. Then try to estimate how much time would it take to clean a specific room and how much time can you invest in the cleaning each day.

For example, the bedroom would require eight hours in total to be neat and clean. You can spend two hours each day for this purpose. This means you'll declutter your bedroom in four days. Add together the time commitment of each room—the kitchen, bathroom, attic, cellar, garage, or what-have-you—for the entire house. Don't be stunned if you get a result of three weeks or a month to finish your decluttering project. That's a sensible timeline if you have a bigger house.

The goal is not to finish as quickly as possible. The goal is to discard the unnecessary, keep the meaningful, and have no regrets later. You may need days or weeks to decide about some items. Take your time.

Okay, you got the theory. Now let's implement what we've learned.

Go to each room and give the clutter a number from one to 10. One is saying that the room is fantastic and very little needs to be discarded. 10 is saying the room is horrible and most of the things need to be considered for discard. Five is somewhere in the middle. It still needs a lot of work, but not as much as your 10 room. You can better prioritize your time if you know what you are getting yourself into.

Here is a cheat sheet for you:

Room _____

1.) *On a scale of 1-10, the clutter level of this room is _____.*
2.) *I will need approximately _____ hours to clean this room.*
3.) *I can invest _____ hours to clean this room.*

Keep your decluttering plan transparent and add as many details as necessary to your decluttering maps to ease your actual work.

You can turn this entire hurdle into a game, if you need extra motivation. Set a deadline for each room and choose which room you want to start with first. Set aside some time for unexpected events. Let's be honest, clearing out places like the garage, attic, and storage room in a day just isn't going to happen, so make sure you plan ahead and add a few extra hours to your initial time estimation.

Don't beat yourself up over these clutter holes. We all have those rooms! One day you have a "junk" drawer, and the next you suddenly have a junk room. That's fine, there's no shame in it.

Once you have your schedule all set in stone and ready to go, it is time to get down to business. As much as we wish that the North Star would grant us our decluttering wish, it hasn't happened yet. Unfortunately, we have to put the work in and declutter ourselves. The nastiest part is that you can't even hire a cleaner to do it because a cleaner doesn't know what you hold dearest, and may have different values on what is needed in a household and whatnot.

One very important step is to come up with a sorting system for the rooms. I love the four-box method of organizing clutter. While you can make your own version of this, it is a simple way to start. One box will be labeled as "unusable," another as "must-have," another as "didn't use for a month," and the final box will be labeled "didn't use it in the past six months." Go through the room and your belongings and sort them into these four boxes. After each room, you can clear out the boxes and start over fresh. I loved using this method because I was shocked at how much stuff hadn't been used for six months. If you would have picked it up and asked me if I wanted the item, I would have said absolutely, but when I saw that I hadn't used it in six months, it gave me a whole new perspective on my belongings.

For the items that you put in the unusable box, there are a few different things you can do with them. Items that are plastic, glass, or paper can be recycled. Find a local recycling center and take it to them. You reduce your carbon footprint, and you can feel good about getting rid of these materials in an ethical way. There are even some local recycling companies who will come to you and help you get rid of your stuff in a recyclable way.

Finally found that iPod touch you lost years ago? Well, don't fret. A little piece of your heart would probably die if you tried to throw that baby in the trash. The good news is, lots of electronics can be recycled too. And the better news is that sometimes they can be recycled for cash! Anytime you can get money for clutter is a great time. One business is called EcoATM. EcoATMs are located in 42 states, and they have over 1,800 kiosks nationwide. If you have one of these close to you, this is a great way to recycle your electronics. Just look up their website to find their nearest location.

If you have some items that could be used by others, donate them. It always feels good to donate to a charity or organization that provides used clothes, toys, and books to families who wouldn't be able to get them otherwise. If you have items in good condition that you just don't want to hold onto, think about donating them. You could also try posting to freecycle.org, a website where people post things for free for people who need them. They come to you, which can save you a trip to the donation store.

For garages especially, there is a ton of stuff that can still be used by others. As the famous saying goes, one man's trash is another man's treasure. Consider holding a garage sale. You'll probably end up with a lot of miscellaneous items that could be sold for some cash. If you start decluttering early enough, you could have quite the turnout. Some neighborhoods even host neighborhood-wide garage sales. This increases the amount of people that come by your sale, and it increases your chances of making money!

For those who just don't want to deal with their stuff, consider renting a dumpster. This is a perfectly suitable and stress-free option. It is a lot cheaper than you think, and it is perfect if you have a lot of stuff to get rid of. The dumpster gets hauled away by the company after you fill it, so it really is an affordable and easy option when decluttering. Consider partnering with a neighbor and renting it together!

Now comes the interesting part. Getting rid of your trash and keeping all the must-have items are a given, but what in the world are you supposed to do with those other two boxes? The "didn't use for one month" and "didn't use for six months" are the trickiest boxes of them all. The stuff in these boxes aren't trash, and they could be useful if you changed a few things. Maybe you need to drop a few pounds to fit in that fancy shirt, or maybe you need to fix the clasp on your favorite necklace after it broke on the night of your sister's bachelorette party (make a note to never drink that much again!). It can be so hard to go through these items and decide whether or not you are truly going to get use out of them enough to justify you keeping them.

For these items, you really have to think about whether or not the item brings you happiness. If you think you are absolutely going to use it in the next month, then keep it. If you feel like you really can't live without it, put it on a trial run. Commit to using it in the next month, and if you don't, then throw it away. You can put these items into a box and put it out in the garage, or in your storage unit. In the next six months, if you find yourself reaching for the items that are stored, take it out. But if you find you still aren't reaching for these items after six months, then there is really no reason to keep the box. It's got to go.

For the box of things you didn't use in the past six months, stop kidding yourself. Those items need to be donated! Now obviously, there are some exceptions to this rule. For one, you don't want to throw out your Christmas decorations. Obviously you didn't use them in the past six months, if December is far away. However, maybe you go through your Christmas decorations and decide what you truly want. Throw away any broken ornaments, get rid of that disco Santa from the 1980s—you know, that type of thing. Same goes for the opposite season clothing. You're going to need both your winter and summer clothes, so don't throw those out just because winter was over six months ago.

This may sound all a bit overwhelming. It actually doesn't take long at all. And remember, hopefully it is a life-lasting process. Hopefully, you won't start hoarding again after going through a big decluttering trauma, and all you'll need from now on will be a quick yearly spring cleaning.

When I decided to declutter, I just dedicated about 30 minutes a day to the process. It took me about a month to get through everything. This might take longer if you have a whole family's worth of belongings to get through, but make everyone else help too!

The basic rule of minimalism is to reduce the number of things you need to comfortably live your life. This is going to look different for everyone. A bachelor is going to need a lot less than a mother of three. It's about simplifying your life. Get rid of the third set of measuring cups in your kitchen, decide on a few pairs of shoes, and keep the rest of your items simple!

Okay, let's take a step back and take a closer look how to clear each room—considering all the challenges and emotional bumps you may encounter. Let's start with your closet. If you are anything like I used to be, your closet probably isn't the best-looking thing ever. I was always envious of those people who have their closets color-coordinated and organized. Seriously, props to those people. They are the people who make the world go 'round.

In all seriousness, cleaning your closet can be therapeutic. You get to go through all your clothes and accessories, and you can get rid of any clothes that might have some negative feelings associated with them.

When you start decluttering your closet, do yourself a favor: Start from the bottom and then work your way up. I know, I know, it is so tempting to start with all of your hanging items, but when you start from the bottom, you get to clear all that stuff out! It's so much easier to organize when you start with all the mess that is the bottom of your closet. That's where people usually shove the things they need the least because the bottom of the closet is the hardest part to reach. Usually the regularly worn clothes are on the shelves which are chest- or eye-level.

Your clothes and shoes do not have minds of their own, so you don't have to worry about them being offended when you get rid of them. It can be tempting to keep a lot of different items, but you have to ask yourself whether they fit, whether they have a problem, and whether or not you've worn them in the past year. It might be the greatest shirt ever, but if you don't wear it, give it away. Some of your items are seasonal, and those you shouldn't get rid—only those that you know for sure you never wear. You can revisit your closet for further downsizing once the season those clothes were meant for returns.

I need to warn you, for sure there are going to be clothes that you keep even though you haven't worn them in forever. But at least try to get rid of everything you can. Once you're finished with the floor, give some TLC to those shelves. Take everything off of them, wipe them down so that they are clean, and then go through everything on your shelves.

When you go to replace the remaining clothes on the shelves, keep it organized. Don't cover up your stuff by stacking folded clothes so high. You want the leftover items to be easily seen so that you will know what you have in your arsenal. It should be as neat as the Louvre! Finish cleaning your closet with everything you have hung up.

You can choose to sort and fold your remaining clothes based on colors. This way, you can compare how many of them are a good match with each other. Which are the shirts you'll probably never wear because they don't match anything else in your closet? Is there anything missing from your wardrobe? (I know this is a counterintuitive question, but you know, it is better to have the essentials that match well with each other than have a hundred random shirts that are not a good fit.)

The next area you could declutter is the bedroom. You sleep in your bedroom, so it needs to be organized and clutter-free. You will actually sleep better when you are not surrounded by your old NSYNC CDs and the blaring TV you fall asleep to every night. Every day starts and finishes in this room, so it should be made into a comfortable sanctuary where you can't resist laying down your head and snuggling to fall asleep. So get cracking, let's do this thing!

Start with the drawers. The nightstand and dresser are probably full of clothing that hasn't seen daylight in years. If you find random items in your drawers like pens, makeup, or anything else, they should go to a different room or get thrown away. Put the items that have not seen sunshine in a year into a throwaway box. You can donate them or get rid of them.

One method that is really helpful for organizing your drawers is to put organizers in them. This is especially true if you are organizing undergarments or socks. This way, those items won't run together and get lost.

Your nightstand and dresser don't need to be decorated with random knickknacks given to you by coworkers of your mother-in-law. If you don't like it, get rid of it immediately. But you also need to be strict on yourself. Allow yourself a few decorations, but don't go over the top. A photo of your loved ones or your favorite place is great, and you can have a lamp or charging station.

Miscellaneous items like your children's' toys and seasonal items can be put somewhere else in the house. These things should not be cluttering your bedroom. Either put it in a storage closet in your house, or rent a storage unit for items that aren't being used.

The next place you spend the most time in is probably the living room. It's where a lot of families get together to play games, watch movies, or just relax at the end of a long day. Toys and books can be strewn across the floor multiple times a day if you have children, and if you're kid-free, you can still have mail and magazines that litter the ottoman and couch. You spend a lot of time in this room, so it might hold a good chunk of your daily clutter.

Decorations aren't usually used too heavily, so they can be great items to donate. Don't forget to clean up the wires that connect to your TV. With DVD players, video game consoles, and Apple TVs, the wires can be unsightly. Combine the cords into one put-together pile to help things look cleaner.

When you reach the kitchen, keep in mind that a clutter-free countertop is much easier to clean. If your kitchen is anything like mine was, it's probably best to split this task up over a few days. You can divide your kitchen into different areas and combat one area at a time. These areas should be organized to have similar items too.

Keep your baking stuff together, your pots and pans together, and silverware by itself.

Don't think that you are exempt from cleaning out your pantry and your refrigerator. Go through both of these things and toss any old or expired food. Get rid of the food you'll never find yourself eating.

Once your kitchen is all wrapped up, consider cleaning up your workspace. If you work from home, that space can definitely benefit from some tender loving care. Desks always seem to get cluttered, no matter what size they are. Remember the desk checks when you were in elementary school? On Fridays, you would scramble to make your desk somewhat clean so you wouldn't get in trouble with the teacher. Think of this as your desk check on steroids. You need to clear out that clutter!

It's time to go through all those papers. If they don't serve a purpose, then what are they doing still hanging around? Get rid of them. You can recycle them, burn them, anything your heart desires. Just get rid of them. Those papers that you *do* need, well, you need to organize them. Put them in a folder or file drawer with labels so you know what they are. You can organize them by date or by category, whatever works best for you. If it is possible to scan those papers and digitize them, that is a great option! You'll still have a copy, but you won't have to store the loose papers.

After you clear out your papers, go through that desk. You are bound to find some random stuff in there. From old chap sticks to 1,000 paperclips, there is going to be a bunch of stuff you can clear out from here. You will work so much more efficiently if you just have your desk and computer with a pad of sticky notes or a journal to keep notes in. Never doubt the power of a clutter-free desk!

Last, but not least, you should go through your bathrooms. If you have more than one bathroom, chances are there isn't too much stuff in the other bathrooms besides your master bathroom. Your master bath is probably going to be the main problem. For women, go through your makeup and hair tools and throw out anything that is expired, old, or broken. Strip it down to your essentials and clear away any perfumes you don't regularly wear. Organize those rubber bands and bobby pins in one spot so you don't keep losing them around the house. For men, go through your hair products and shaving products. Throw out gunky razors, creams, and gels you no longer use.

Then you can tackle the remaining stuff with all the rest of the bathrooms. For example, go through all the bathroom towels. Now is the perfect opportunity to throw out those torn or ripped hand towels. Go through the medicine cabinets, cleaning supplies, and everything else that makes up your bathrooms. Try to get rid of decorations in the bathroom that are unnecessary. You don't spend a ton of time in the bathroom, so this should be the easiest room to declutter. Reorganize everything in your bathroom so that it is neat and orderly. Invest in some nice storage baskets to keep everything in its place.

After you have decluttered your home, you'll probably feel like a champ, as you should. However, you might feel like you have really torn everything down in the house. You may even think that it looks barren. If so, you can always jazz up your house with a little, and I really mean *just a bit*, of decoration.

Feel free to repaint your walls in a color that is appealing to you. This adds a new element to your home without creating more clutter. Whites or light grays are modern and comforting, and they also increase the natural light in a room. Colder colors like blue or black can be comforting to some individuals, while others may opt for warmer colors like deep oranges or reds. Whatever you feel comfortable in should be the deciding factor.

The list of duplicated items

You can use the same paper you used to estimate the time you'd need to clean each room. Turn the page and start taking inventory of what you have in each given room. For example: one pair of scissors, two nail clippers, one hair dryer…

Then compare the inventory of each room. If you discover that you have five nail clippers and three pairs of scissors, maybe you should say goodbye to some of them. I know, I know. What if you don't find one of the nail clippers? It is comforting to know that you have four others. This is the point of decluttering: to find a place for everything. Not finding something shouldn't be an option because everything will have its well-known place. If you don't feel like you can find anything in two seconds after decluttering, that means you didn't do a profound job. I would advise you to resume the decluttering and organizing process and take as much time as needed to find a place for each item.

You made it clean, keep it clean

The struggle is real. No one enjoys cleaning their house, let's be honest. Okay, okay, I'm sure there are some people out there who like cleaning, but I am not one of them. Anytime I can limit my cleaning time is good for me. When there's less stuff in the house, there's less stuff to clean!

If you struggle with keeping your house clean, don't worry about it. It is a common problem. Once you declutter, you have to try really hard to keep it clean so you don't end up back at square one. That leads us to the first thing we are going to talk about: making a wise decluttering decision.

Let's talk about the 80/20 rule. There's an 80/20 rule that applies to a lot of different things in life, but I'm specifically talking about how it relates to minimalism. For example, your closet. Did you know you regularly wear 20% of the all the clothes you possess 80% of the time? And it doesn't stop there. This holds true for almost everything you own.

You have to ask yourself, "What value do these items bring into my life?" Or even better, "What value do I lose in my life if I throw them away?"

Let's see, if you get rid of the random, mismatched pieces of silverware and measuring cup sets, then you are left with more drawer space, a cleaner and clutter-free kitchen, and you're left with only the nicest of your silverware and measuring cups. Sounds like a win-win, right? When you are deciding what to keep and what to throw away, keep this little tidbit in mind: You're probably not going to miss those things. If you do, you should have kept track of the pieces you lost in the first place.

You also have to ask yourself when you used the item last. If you happen upon a DVD that you're shocked you have, you probably don't need it. Same goes for the rest of your stuff. Finally found that T-shirt you've been missing for three months? Well, you did just fine without it for three months, so you can live without it for the rest of time. We talked about these things in the previous chapter. Let's see how to keep clean all that remains.

One of the greatest ways to keep your house looking clean is learning to keep similar things in groups. Keeping items you frequently use together in the same place just makes the most sense. This is how they organize big warehouses. Items that are purchased together often get placed right next to each other. It makes it easy and simple when you need to grab these items. It can help you keep your home organized, and you'll never have to spend hours looking for that specific blanket if you keep all your blankets in one place.

I'm a big fan of storage boxes. You can get all kinds of sizes for different purposes. For example, I keep all my kitchen ingredients in boxes. I put flour, sugar, starch, salt, etc. in a transparent storage box. This way, when I dust once a month, I only need to dust the box. It is also easier to dust my kitchen cabinet; I don't need to move 20 tiny ingredients. All I need to do is take out the storage box, clean the cabinet, put the box back, and done. You can do this with almost everything you own: DVDs, pillows-blankets, toiletries, makeup stuff, large kitchen items, etc.

I'm convinced that the messiest places in my home used to involve flat surfaces. Seriously, that kitchen countertop was a magnet for all my messy and miscellaneous items. My mail got put there, I kept my calendar there, and even my blender and mixer ended up taking room on my kitchen counter. Soon enough, it started to look like I tried to make a kitchen-sized model of the Rocky Mountains. Piles were all over the place, and man, that was hard to even look at, not to mention working on it.

I pledged to keep all my flat surfaces clean, so I adopted the high five rule. This means that only five items can coexist on any flat surface at the same time. These items can be the five most decorative things for the living room, the most frequently used items for the kitchen and bathroom, and so on. For my high five, I cleaned everything up, threw away the newspapers as old as time, and then I designated a drawer with a tiny storage box for those wretched bills I had to keep.

I bet that you too struggle with flat surfaces. Whether it's your kitchen counter, your nightstand, or your dining room table, high five it

Chapter 7: Organizing Tips

Now it is time to really buckle down and organize the remaining items you decided to keep. If everything in your house has its place, then you will not only feel good, but you'll be more likely to keep it clean and organized in the future! I've collected some tips for every part of your home.

First things first, let's organize that closet of yours. Organizing your clothes can be a dreadful experience, but it shouldn't have to be! One tip that really helped me was to stagger my shoes. You put one shoe facing forward and the other shoe facing backward. It sounds strange, but it is a simple hack that can help free up some much needed room in your closet.

A great way to help make your closet look neat and organized is to invest in some high-quality matching hangers. It's time to retire the 50 shades of broken hangers you have in your closet. Get some hangers that won't break. Your clothes deserve good-looking hangers. You don't need to spend all your savings on hangers, of course. What I did was a little DIY magic. I bought a bunch of plain, black hangers and I painted dots on them with my nail polish. I have a lot of nail polish shades, and man, they are all very important, so didn't discard them. Luckily, this meant I could paint polka pots on each hanger, matching the color of the cloth I hung on it. If you are a man who doesn't like polka dots and nail polish, just keep all the hangers black. It is elegant and stylish.

Shelf brackets can also help you fit clothing better into your closet. They are like small triangles you drill into your wall that stick out so you can hang clothes on them. They are perfect for hanging jeans so they never get wrinkled, and you don't have to fold them! Win-win, right?

But hey, I know everything can't be hung up in your closet. Eventually, you're going to have to fold some stuff. Let me introduce you to the Marie Kondo way of folding clothes. Not only is it super-efficient, but it is going to clear up so much space in your closet. Since the instructions are sometimes hard to follow, I inserted a link to a YouTube video at the end of each folding description.

Trousers and Jeans

If you don't want to hang, but rather fold your jeans, try out this method. Lay out your jeans so that they are flat in front of you. Take the left leg and fold it over the right leg. Then fold in the crotch area so it is a nice and smooth parallel line from the waistband to the ankle. Fold in half, then half it again, then one more time! The jeans will stand up straight so they can be stacked on your shelf. Don't make a vertical stacking; rather, try to position your folded things in horizontally. This way the items will be more accessible. If you need the jeans from the bottom, you won't destroy that foot-long tower of clothes, and yes, you also can't stuff as many things in your closet this way.

Video:
https://www.youtube.com/watch?v=Vds4_L7RMUs. Video credit: Sarah Sky.

T-shirts

For your T-shirts, start with the shirt laying out in front of you. Fold over one side of the shirt so that it is lying a third of the way across the front. Fold the sleeve backward in half. Repeat on the other side. You should end up with a perfectly straight rectangle at this point. Then fold the shirt in half, then a third of the way, then in half again, and you're finished! Your shirts should end up standing up the same way the jeans did. The Marie Kondo folding method is pretty simple once you have one garment down. They are very similar.

Video:
https://www.youtube.com/watch?v=Lpc5_1896ro. Video credit: Ebury Reads.

Socks and underwear

For socks and underwear, get ready for a new kind of folding that is going to better organize your drawers! Ever lose a sock? Of course you have, and it's horrible! If you fold your socks with this method, you'll never lose another one.

Lay the matching pair of socks one on top of the other. You're going to fold the sock almost in half, keeping the toe about an inch away from the top. Then fold in the folded end so that it lines up with the center. Fold the sock in half, and they should stand upright.

With underwear, start your fold with the crotch area. Fold it upward toward the waistband. Then fold each side of the underwear into the center. Fold it once more in half, and you're finished![vii]

Video: https://www.youtube.com/watch?v=tglp9eWQEhY. Video credit: *New York Magazine*.

Marie Kondo's way of folding is mind-blowingly simple, yet amazing. Everything in your closet will stand up straight like little soldiers. You're left with a cleaner-looking and more spacious closet.

Now that the closet is done, it is time to organize your kitchen.

The most important thing about your kitchen is that it should stay clean and sanitized. Make sure that you have easily wipeable countertops. There is so much bacteria that can be hanging around in the kitchen, so it is important to be able to clean it every day. By taking away the clutter that is normally in your kitchen, you can clean much easier and faster.

Quick tip for quick cleaning: I use cleaning wipes to swoosh-swoosh through my counter tops every day. Use antibacterial wet napkins, not baby wipes! Some of my friends use baby wipes to clean everything from the toilet to the kitchen. I often tell them that they just cleaned the backside of the bacteria now. Don't forget to go through the sanitized area with a clean, wet cloth (wet with water only) two to three minutes after you sanitized. You don't want to eat off the chemicals the sanitizer is made out of.

Set up your kitchen in such a way that you can remember the place for everything you keep in it. This way you won't stand puzzled for five minutes, wondering where the salt is. Keep the most important and most frequently used items close together and near the oven, stove, or in the closest area on the shelves. Store items together that you use in conjunction with one another a lot. For example, your wooden spoons and spatulas could be stored in the same area.

A great way to store your measuring tools would be to hang them up on a corkboard. You can get corkboard for pennies on the dollar, and if you add hooks to it, you can put it on your pantry door or in a cabinet and hang up your measuring tools. This way you don't have to sift through a bunch of drawers to find the measuring cup.

If you love a clean and organized pantry, consider investing in some containers as I mentioned before. You can also buy some labels down at the dollar store and help yourself label what each container keeps. It can look very modern, depending on the labels you use, and it helps you to remember what you have in the particular box. Speaking of labeling, do not forget to label everything in your freezer. Seriously, it makes life so much easier if you put labels on the things you freeze. You'll know exactly what you have and what its expiry date is.

If you're short on space in your kitchen, command hooks are your new best friend. You can easily hang your pots and pans, mixer attachments, and anything else that has a spot to hang. It can free up some much-needed cabinet or pantry space. There are so many great ways to organize your kitchen, but just remember, less is more.

When you're moving on to the bathrooms, make sure they are practically clutter-free. I don't even have to tell you how gross bathrooms can get, so they should be as minimalist as possible. This means that you should be organizing as much as you can to fit everything in there. If you're short on space in the bathroom, you're one of the millions of Americans who have a tiny bathroom.

Consider installing one of those wall cabinets. They are very easy to attach to the wall, and they can be put above the toilet for those small half-baths that hold nothing in them.

However, if you are in a rental or you don't want to install something on your walls, consider getting a cart for items like cotton balls, Q-tips, and towels. Carts can be bought at places like IKEA, or you could totally make one yourself! It's a fun project for a rainy day, that's for sure.

If you have children, you probably have bath toys strewn across the bathroom like nobody's business. It's time to get rid of those. Well, you don't have to literally get rid of the toys, but you should put them away. It can be tough trying to give your kids a bath and then clean up the toys after. A great way to keep things clean is using a suction cup hook on the side of the bathtub with a mesh bag. You can throw all the toys into the mesh bag and then hang it up on the wall so it is out of the way when you finally get to have that shower to yourself. No mom or dad should ever have to ruin their shower by stepping on some plastic duckling.

Don't forget to wipe the toilet with sanitizer (and then a wet cloth), and especially those surfaces children can reach easily. The toilet is the second (arguably the first) most unhygienic place in your home after the kitchen. Keep the bacteria away from it.

Thankfully, though, the bathroom isn't seen too often by other people. At least, not your master bathroom. The room that is seen by people is your living room. It is called the *living* room for a reason! We spend most of our time there throughout the day, and it has the most opportunity to become a tornado-torn room. Once you get rid of most of the clutter, you should be left with a nice, clean living room.

Invest in furniture that is practical, durable, and cozy. Throw your favorite blanket on the ottoman and display some of your favorite photos on the wall. Keeping the coffee table and side tables clear of photo frames will make them easy to clean. You should also try to conceal the wires behind your TV, your lamps, and anything else that might have a bulky cord. Your goal with this room should be to keep everything looking sharp and neat.

It's time to tackle the real problem. How many of you have decluttered your garage? Yes, I see you there! The garage is not a place to hold your clutter. I get it, the room is big, it is technically an empty space outside, and only the car and some bugs see what's going around there. I know the garage seems to offer the perfect solution to those who don't really want to discard items. "I just box up my clutter and bring it to my garage. This way it won't be in the house, but I'll have my things. Just in case my corkscrew breaks in 10 years, I will have one extra in the garage..." My friend, you are in trouble if you can't buy a new corkscrew in 10 years.

Jokes aside, garages aren't a one-size-fits-all type of space. There are plenty of people who have no problem with garage space, and there are others who can never have enough garage space. It also depends on your family. Maybe you have a husband who is a huge outdoorsman and keeps his gear in the garage, or maybe your husband is a mechanic with a million and one tools. Maybe your children have a ton of bikes that never seem to stay standing on their kickstand. It's time to put an end to the misery!

First things first, discard the items that are broken, you never use, and don't need. Then organize what you do need. You can't throw out your kids' bikes, but you can hang them from the ceiling with an industrial-strength hook. This can free up so much space, and it keeps the bikes off the ground so only you can get them down when they need them. If you have a bunch of storage bins, then you should take a weekend to build some shelving for them. It's actually a very easy project, and it makes stacking bins so much safer.

Take note of all the wall space in your garage. It takes only minutes to set up some good shelving, and it's so easy to store all those miscellaneous items like bug spray, oil for your car, and your toolbox. This includes installing a tool rack for your shovels and rakes. You should get everything off the floor that you can. Of course, you don't need to invest as much effort in your garage as you do in your living areas when you declutter. Just make the garage space (or attic, or cellar) functional, transparent, and safe. Most household accidents happen in the garage.

If you have kids who love to play sports, congratulations! It is so much fun to watch your kids excel at sports, but it is even more fun when their sports gear is organized. This is especially true for balls. How many times have you almost run over that soccer ball or basketball? Too many times, probably. Make a ball jail for them! All you need is some plywood and bungee cords. Build a rectangular frame, then tie bungee cords across the front so your kids can reach in and grab the balls, but the balls won't fall out on their own.

If you don't have a garage, there's always a way to store those items you need. Get a small shed to put in the backyard to help you keep your shelving organized and secure. You won't regret it.

Chapter 8: Holiday Special

There's no doubt about it—holidays are the best time of the year! There is so much happiness and magic surrounding us on Thanksgiving, Christmas, 4th of July, and let's not forget the amazing decorations we all pull out to make our houses look beautiful. It truly is an incredible time. However, holidays are also a trap for those who want to live a more minimalist lifestyle. There are too many cute decorations to say no to, and between the ugly sweater parties and the endless movies, it can be a bit stressful to say no too many times, or to not say no and get anxious about the accumulating clutter.

Holidays are the time of year when I get to go home for an extended period of time. I love seeing my family, but I hate seeing everything they have hoarded over the past half a year. I make it my personal mission every July and December to discard the useless things they have collected.

Before Christmas or the 4th of July happens, we stockpile useless stuff in our homes from the other holidays like Halloween and Thanksgiving. There are a ton of decorations sitting in our garages, and we make it even harder when we start buying endless amounts of new décor. Then the holiday comes and a whole new batch of gifts, turkeys, fireworks, and whatnot show up at our door.

Simplify your holidays by decluttering before them this year. No, this does not mean get rid of your Christmas or Thanksgiving decorations, or your "I Love the USA" T-shirt. That would be an abomination! But you should go through them. There are probably some broken decorations and décor you have in your storage box. Don't try to fix that cheap plastic ornament—just throw it away. Decorations that you no longer like should definitely go.

Donate your old decorations that are no longer getting any use. There are plenty of people out there who would be happy to take these decorations off your hands. Organizations that help those in need are a great place to donate to. I have donated the past few years to these organizations, and it makes me feel really good about the items I am purging. I have decided to follow what Peter Walsh says: "If everything is special, then nothing is special." This saying is so true. We have to appreciate the decorations we have by giving away the small things we don't like any longer.

One rule I have recently applied to my life is Santa's Rule. Its philosophy is "get one, toss two." I not only adopt this rule on Christmas, but on each holiday. For each gift you buy or receive (and keep), you have to toss two other items. If you buy a new cookie cutter, then it is time to get rid of two older cookie cutters. This simple rule can help keep your house looking clean and clutter-free. Plus you get to donate, which always feels better than to receive!

This exercise is especially good for kids. If your kids receive a new pair of pajamas, try donating two pairs they have outgrown. Whether you throw out raggedy old items or you donate them, it is a good way to declutter your home. You can also teach your kids how to declutter and give selflessly with this exercise; when they get something, they should choose one or two toys to give to other kids who might need them more.

Another fun way to declutter is to take the mailing box challenge. If you're anything like me, you probably love to order presents online. Unfortunately, this means you end up with a bunch of boxes in your house. While you could reuse them or recycle them, there's an even better way to make them useful. You can set a goal to fill every mailing box you get with items that you are going to donate this year! Get your family involved and see how much you can get rid of.

However, holidays shouldn't be all about decluttering. Now it is time to balance out the scales. Holidays are magical for a reason. They bring the family together, so participate in the magic. Let loose and eat those five gingerbread cookies, the turkey, or the hot dog. Decorate your home with your favorite decorations.

Commit to being kind. This extends to more than just being kind to others. Be kind to yourself too. Do something nice for someone else. My family always likes to deliver baked goods to neighbors, and we have put together small hygiene kits for homeless people as well. These small acts of kindness teach our family that we should be kind to everyone.

But unfortunately, all good things must come to an end, even holidays. When you go to pick up your post-celebration mess, make sure you do it correctly. Commit to putting away your décor items in the most organized way possible. So many of us are sad that the holiday season is over, so we throw our decorations into a box and say we will worry about them later.

This year, sort through your stuff and put it away correctly. You want to get rid of items you are not going to use, and this includes horrible presents that relatives may have given you. Don't let these gifts become a burden in your home. You can either donate and get rid of the presents without a second thought, or you can try to exchange them in the store they were bought for something you actually like. You could always re-gift the present if it was good. Sometimes we end up with duplicates of gifts, and there's nothing we can do about it. Perhaps you could stick it in your closet to re-gift to someone for a birthday present later on this year. Just remember to scribble a note saying who gave you which present so that you don't end up re-gifting the present to the same person. That would be awkward.

Or, if you want to get very creative, consider having a post-holiday gift exchange. Make it full of White Elephants gifts and have a good laugh with your closest friends about the things you received this Christmas, Thanksgiving, or any other holiday you celebrate. You'll get rid of your clutter, share some fun times with your friends, and hey, you might just end up loving a gift that someone else hated!

Last, but not least, if you end up with some books you don't need or have already read, consider swapping them out for something new and better. You can get on sites like Paperback Swap and Book Mooch to swap out your book for something you haven't read. It's a great way to stay current on your reading without it becoming too overwhelming for your small bookshelf.

Final Thoughts

I would like to thank you, dear future mess-less reader, for bearing with me to the sweet end of this book. Hopefully your palms are itching to discard your clutter and organize your home into something that fills your heart with joy and satisfaction.

Remember, at the end of the day, the most important takeaway of this book is that the best-organized home is the one you love living in. Therefore, downsize, declutter, and discard just as much as it makes your heart happy. Something must be bothering you in your home, otherwise you wouldn't have picked up this book. Find out what's the matter and start acting on it.

Feel free to share your organizing success stories with me via email at michellembooks@gmail.com. Also, if you have any better tips or personal tricks for decluttering and organizing, send them to me. Who knows? Maybe I'll feature them in my next book.

I'm truly honored that you read my book. Thank you for your time and support! I'm happy I could sit by your side for a few hours and connect with you through these pages. Have an amazing life!

Yours,
Michelle

P.S.: If you liked my book or you have any constructive criticism, let others (and me) know it!

Visit https://www.amazon.com/review/create-review?asin=PUTASIN HERE# to leave a review. Thank you for helping me improve!

Other Books

If you liked my book, you might like these, too:

Why Do You Do This?

Mindfulness

Minimalist Money Makeover

Unhooked

Reference

Brennan, Siofra. *Would YOU try Swedish death cleaning? How asking yourself if loved ones will want your things after you're DEAD could beat clutter for good*. The Daily Mail. 2017.
http://www.dailymail.co.uk/femail/article-4982420/Would-try-Swedish-death-cleaning.html

Edwards, Catherine. *'Swedish death-cleaning is something we should all think about – and enjoy.'* The Local. 2017.
https://www.thelocal.se/20171017/swedish-death-cleaning-decluttering-book-grandma-elderly

Kondo, Marie. *The Life Changing Magic Of Tidying Up*. Ten Speed Press. 2014

Magnusson, Margareta. *The Gentle Art of Swedish Death Cleaning: How to Free Yourself and Your Family from a Lifetime of Clutter.* Scribner. 2017. https://www.amazon.com/Gentle-Art-Swedish-Death-Cleaning/dp/1501173243

Matthews, Lyndsey. What Is Hygge? Everything You Need To Know About The Danish Lifestyle Trend. Country Living. 2017. http://www.countryliving.com/life/a41187/what-is-hygge-things-to-know-about-the-danish-lifestyle-trend/

Millburn, Fields, Joshua. Nicodemus, Ryan. *What Is Minimalism?* The Minimalists. 2017. https://www.theminimalists.com/minimalism/

Sullivan, Meg. *Trouble in paradise: UCLA book enumerates challenges faced by middle-class L.A. families.* UCLA. 2012.

http://newsroom.ucla.edu/releases/trouble-in-paradise-new-ucla-book

Endnotes

---

[i] Millburn, Fields, Joshua. Nicodemus, Ryan. *What Is Minimalism?* The Minimalists. 2017.
https://www.theminimalists.com/minimalism/

[ii] Matthews, Lyndsey. What Is Hygge? Everything You Need To Know About The Danish Lifestyle Trend. Country Living. 2017.
http://www.countryliving.com/life/a41187/what-is-hygge-things-to-know-about-the-danish-lifestyle-trend/

[iii] Brennan, Siofra. *Would YOU try Swedish death cleaning? How asking yourself if loved ones will want your things after you're DEAD could beat clutter for good.* The Daily Mail. 2017.
http://www.dailymail.co.uk/femail/article-4982420/Would-try-Swedish-death-cleaning.html

[iv] Edwards, Catherine. *'Swedish death-cleaning is something we should all think about – and enjoy.'* The Local. 2017.
https://www.thelocal.se/20171017/swedish-death-cleaning-decluttering-book-grandma-elderly

[v] Magnusson, Margareta. *The Gentle Art of Swedish Death Cleaning: How to Free Yourself and*

Your Family from a Lifetime of Clutter. Scribner. 2017. https://www.amazon.com/Gentle-Art-Swedish-Death-Cleaning/dp/1501173243

[vi] Sullivan, Meg. *Trouble in paradise: UCLA book enumerates challenges faced by middle-class L.A. families.* UCLA. 2012. http://newsroom.ucla.edu/releases/trouble-in-paradise-new-ucla-book

[vii] Kondo, Marie. *The Life Changing Magic Of Tidying Up.* 10 Speed Press. 2014

www.ingramcontent.com/pod-product-compliance
Lightning Source LLC
Chambersburg PA
CBHW020105240426
43661CB00002B/43